Contents

What is bullying?

Bullying affects many young people. Bullying means being deliberately horrible, threatening or even violent towards someone who cannot defend themselves.

There are many different types of bullying. These fall into three main areas: physical, verbal and psychological.

Physical bullying involves touching someone in some way. This could include hitting, kicking, pushing, spitting or beating someone up. It could also involve breaking or stealing someone's possessions. At school, bullies often take people's lunch money or books.

Verbal bullying means saying nasty things to people. This could be name-calling, mimicking, taunting or making someone look stupid. Some bullies use this type of bullying on people who look different from them. For example, people who have a different colour skin.

▼ Bullies, being cowards, often form into a gang to frighten their victim.

WE'RE TALKING ABOUT
BULLYING

ANNE CHARLISH

WAYLAND

Series editor: Catherine Baxter
Series designer: John Christopher
Book editor: Carron Brown
Designer: Malcolm Walker, Kudos Design
Consultant: Pauline Hasler, Anti-Bullying Campaign

This edition published in 1999 by Wayland Publishers Ltd

First published in 1997 by Wayland Publishers Ltd
61 Western Road, Hove, East Sussex, BN3 1JD, England

Find Wayland on the internet at http://www.wayland.co.uk

British Library Cataloguing in Publication Data

Charlish, Anne
We're Talking About Bullying
1. Bullying – Juvenile literature
I. Title II. Bullying
371.5'8
ISBN 0-7502-2577 7

Typeset by Malcolm Walker, Kudos Design, England
Printed and bound by Canale & C.S.p.A, Turin

Picture Acknowledgements
ACE Photo Agency/ (Megasnaps) 4, 10; Tony Stone (David Young-Wolff) 20; Wayland Picture Library 5, 6, 7, 11, 16, 19, 28/ (Danny Allmark) Cover/ (APM Studios) 14/ (Chris Fairclough) title page, 8,9, 12, 13, 21, 22, 23, 24, 26, 27, 29/ (Skjold) 18/ (Zak Waters) 15; Zefa 17,25.
Most of the people featured in this book are models

Psychological bullying means picking on someone without saying anything to them or touching them. Instead, the bully hurts their victim by not speaking to them at all or not including them in the things they do, giving them nasty looks, sending horrible notes, spreading rumours, hiding possessions or following them home from school.

Being bullied is a horrible experience and you will know if it is happening to you. It is not bullying if someone pushes you, just once and clearly not on purpose. If, however, someone pushes you every breaktime at school, and you know that it is not by accident, this person is bullying you.

Some bullies try to cover up their behaviour when someone challenges them about it. They may say: 'I was only joking', or 'I was just teasing, I didn't mean it', or 'It was only a bit of fun'.

▲ Bullies often try to steal or hide people's food and possessions.

Bullying behaviour is a form of aggression. Bullies want to prove that they are bigger and better than the people they pick on. They want their victims to be scared of them. They also want people to look up to them.

When, where and how often does bullying happen?

Bullying often happens at a time and a place where it will not be seen by teachers or parents. This could be during breaktimes and when travelling to and from school. Bullies also target their victims on the stairs, between lessons and in the toilets. They may also say nasty things and give nasty looks during lessons in the classroom. In boarding schools, bullying attacks happen a lot. The children cannot go home to get away from them, and nowhere is safe.

It is difficult to know how many children are being bullied and how many are bullies. Children often do not want to tell their teachers and parents what is happening.

◄ It is always best to tell a friend or your teacher if you are being bullied, then something can be done about it.

▲ If you are bullied every day, you can become very lonely and sad. You may feel that school has become a very frightening place to be.

Bullying is very common, especially at primary school, and many children have gone through it. It is very harmful. If you are being bullied, tell someone about it. Nothing can be done to stop bullies if no one knows what they are doing.

It is thought that up to one million pupils in the UK are involved in bullying, either as a bully or as a victim. As many as 360,000 children are bullied every week at primary school. About one-third of girls and one-quarter of boys feel afraid of going to school because they are scared of being bullied. The organization ChildLine, which gives advice to young people who call them, had more than 8,000 calls concerned with bullying in one year alone. Some children are bullied nearly every day. They live their lives in fear and misery because of it. They become unhappy, lose their self-confidence and find it difficult to concentrate on their schoolwork.

Andrew's story

Andrew is eleven years old. He bullies another boy called John at school.

Whenever Andrew does anything bad to John, the other boys in the class think he's really tough. It makes him feel good and powerful. But, inside, Andrew doesn't feel tough. He feels awful about stealing John's lunch every day and taunting him on the bus home.

Andrew knows John will be going home and seeing both his parents and having a nice tea.

Andrew feels jealous of John's life. Andrew's mum is always late home from work, so she has given him a key to let himself into the house. Andrew's dad left home, though he doesn't really know why. His mum told him that his dad did not want to live with her any more because he did not love her. Andrew misses his dad a lot.

▼ Andrew and his friends made John's life a misery by stealing his lunch at break and picking on him all the time.

One day, Andrew is called in to see the head teacher. She tells Andrew that what he's doing to John is very bad and cruel. She says that Andrew is making him ill and very unhappy. The head teacher knows that Andrew is having problems at home. She says that having problems cannot be used as a reason to be cruel to another boy. Andrew's behaviour will not make his dad come back. She says that if she hears that he ever bullies anyone again, he will be in very serious trouble.

▲ Andrew knows that he is in serious trouble when his head teacher calls him into her office to warn him to stop bullying other, smaller children.

This upsets Andrew, and makes him feel stupid and guilty. He knew deep down that it was wrong to pick on someone who was weaker than him. Andrew stops bullying John and tries to feel better about his life. He asks his mum to arrange for him to see his dad more often, which makes Andrew feel happier.

Why do people bully?

Most bullying starts at nursery school and continues through to primary school. Boys usually go for violent types of bullying though sometimes girl bullies do too. Girl bullies are more likely to send nasty notes and spread rumours, taunt and tease. Both boy and girl bullies do not allow their victims into their group of friends.

▲ It is more frightening for the victim when both boys and girls bully together in a gang.

Bullies often feel insecure and worried, but they want people to think they are tough. They think that the way to do this is to act aggressively. When the bully is alone, rather than in a gang,

▶ This boy is being bullied by his older brothers. The boy may become a bully himself out of revenge for what his brothers are doing to him at home.

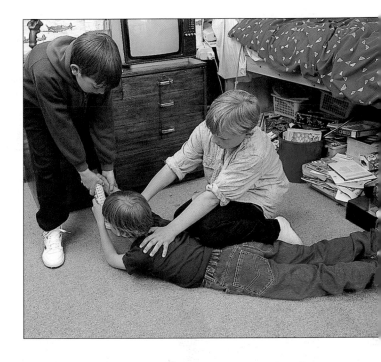

there is no need to be tough. Bullies like to have people watching them. They may even be scared to act tough without other people around to watch them bullying.

Many bullies think they have to be forceful in order to get what they want. They want other people to feel as bad and as helpless as they do. But because bullies usually pick on someone smaller and weaker than them, they do not achieve anything.

There are many reasons why people become bullies. They may think that aggression can help them have their own way because they see it happen at home. For example, a bully may have parents who fight and argue at home, or he or she may even be

bullied by older brothers and sisters, or older children at school. Bullies like to feel powerful, popular and in control.

Bullies should ask themselves how they would feel if they were treated in the same way as they treat other children.

Andrew can see now that he made John feel really bad. He knew that John sometimes tried to get a different bus from him. John never even had anything to eat for lunch. Andrew knew that if it had happened to him, he would have been very unhappy.

Katy's story

Katy was bullied every day at her primary school when she was about ten years old. Usually, about ten of the people in her class, both girls and boys, ganged up on Katy. They used to close in about her in the playground and say nasty things that really hurt her. This happened day after day.

One day, Katy and her class were in the hall for break because it was raining. The boys grabbed hold of Katy and dragged her up

◀ Katy was afraid to tell her class teacher what was happening to her at breaktimes. It is always better to tell someone than to suffer in silence.

and down the hall. Katy let them do it, because they thought it was funny. She thought she was making them laugh, but Katy can see now they were just making fun of her. Katy was bumped and bruised all over. It really hurt.

During lessons, Katy would be asked questions by the teacher. She was good at her schoolwork. Katy knew that once outside, the teasing would begin. They would call her 'swot' and 'teacher's pet'. Katy felt bad about being able to answer questions in class and being made fun of.

Being bullied caused Katy a lot of embarrassment. She just wanted to hide at breaktimes. Katy felt as if she had no friends. Her mum told Katy to stick up for herself. But Katy felt that she could not defend herself against ten other children.

▲ Katy often felt she would only be safe from the bullies if she hid at breaktimes and lunchtime.

Why do people get bullied?

Anyone who is seen to be different, or who is seen to be weaker in any way, risks being bullied. Bullies often go for children who look different or who are very shy and quiet. Even having a different accent or an unusual name may be enough to start a bully teasing you.

Sometimes, children are bullied without realizing what is happening. This happens when someone really wants to be part of a group of friends. He or she may let the children in that group tell them what to do, even if it means giving up their lunch or their pocket money so they can be popular. This is a type of bullying.

◀ A bully may try to pick on anyone whose race, religion or culture is different from his or hers.

Some children may feel that it is worth being bullied in order to make contact with older or more popular children. They would rather be bullied than ignored. Some children may be bullied by children who are jealous of them. For example, the child could be better at schoolwork or have a family with a lot of money.

Bullies like to pick on people who show they are weak in some way. Unfortunately, if a bully

▲ Happy and friendly children do not feel the need to bully others. They enjoy their friendships and they value their friends.

picks on someone every day, their confidence falls, causing the bully to pick on them even more. If you have confidence in yourself and are happy with who you are and the friends that you have, you will probably escape being bullied.

The effects of bullying

The effects of bullying can be extremely serious. About ten children each year kill themselves because their lives have been made so miserable by a bully.

The effects of bullying include: feeling afraid all the time; becoming depressed and sad; being unable to sleep or having nightmares; performing badly at school; not wanting to go to school; not eating; stomach-aches and headaches; asthma; eczema; losing your self-confidence; and even being tempted to bully others in revenge.

Some children develop signs of depression that are serious enough to need professional help from a doctor or psychiatrist.

One of the most horrible, long-term effects of bullying is that you gradually lose your self-confidence and you stop believing in yourself. Without this belief, you begin to feel unhappy about yourself and you enjoy life less.

One child who killed himself in 1996 at the age of thirteen wrote in his diary

'I shall remember this for eternity and will never forget.
***Monday:** My money was taken.*
***Tuesday:** Names called.*
***Wednesday:** My uniform torn.*
***Thursday:** My body pouring with blood.*
***Friday:** It's ended.*
***Saturday** (thought to be the day he died): Freedom'*

◄ Being bullied can lead to someone feeling frightened all the time and being unable to trust other people.

Your schoolwork may begin to suffer. It is hard to do work when you are more worried about what the bully will do to you next.

Many children who are bullied do not realize that parents and teachers know about bullying in schools. Do not feel alone if you are being bullied. It happens to many children. Do not believe that you alone have been singled out for this cruel and hurtful treatment. Do not think there must be something peculiar, horrible, stupid or unattractive about you that makes the bully pick on you. Try to feel good about yourself and try not to let the bully get the better of you.

The longer you are bullied, the more time it takes to recover from it. If you do not do anything about the bullying, the bully will continue to destroy your self-confidence and your life.

Stopping a bully

In order to stop someone from bullying you, you need to understand why they do it and why you react like you do. You need to learn to understand your feelings about bullying, and the bully's own feelings as well.

It is normal to feel bad when someone bullies you. Anyone would. The important thing, however, is to try not to show

▲ If you are being bullied, make sure you tell someone about it so that the bullies will be stopped from picking on others. Show the bullies that you are confident and unafraid and, soon, they should leave you alone.

that they have upset you. You must also realize that just because you feel bad at the moment, this does not mean that you are bad.

The bully wants you to be upset. Your best defence is to ignore the bully, even if it is hard to do. If he or she hits you or calls you names, walk away. If someone sends you a nasty note, or breaks something of yours, just do your best to ignore it.

This is very difficult to do, but it does work. A bully will give up when he or she sees that you are strong. Also, tell someone you trust about the bullying, or they will only pick on someone else. They must not get away with it.

Remind yourself that most bullies are unhappy and feel bad about themselves. They may have problems at home. They may be bad at their schoolwork. They may not have any real friends. People do not usually like bullies.

◄ Learning to be confident in yourself is an important part of growing up. A bully does not usually go for someone who they think is strong.

▶ Concentrate on the things you enjoy and are good at, for example sports or drawing, and try to feel good about yourself.

You must tell yourself that the bullies act the way they do out of revenge and jealousy. A bully has no right to hurt you, and you do not deserve to be the victim of his or her anger. Try to feel good about yourself. It might help to make a list about what you think are your good points. If you feel happy with yourself, it may give you the self-confidence and respect you need to walk away from a bully.

You will soon come to the point where you feel able to look at the bully and think to yourself 'How dare you speak to me in that way!' and walk away with your head held high. If you have to speak, do so clearly, calmly and confidently.

Bullies are less likely to go for people who are strong, fun, friendly, kind, thoughtful and confident. You can think yourself into being like this, even if you do not feel like that kind of person. Think positively about yourself, your home, your family, your schoolwork and your achievements. Is there something you are really good at? Concentrate on these things and try to look after yourself.

As your self-confidence grows, you will find it easier to make friends. You will soon believe that anyone would be glad to have you as their friend. Remember that making friends is something that takes a bit of time and effort. You cannot expect others to do everything. Once the bully sees that you are happy and that you have good friends, he or she will be much less likely to target you. Do not forget that bullies are unhappy people. They are frightened and cruel, and they probably do not like themselves much.

◄ Katy became really good friends with one or two people who she really liked. It took time to get to know them, but she's a lot happier now.

How to stop bullying others

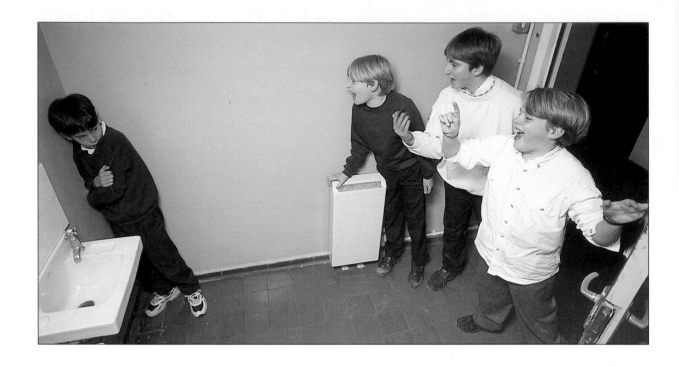

Lawrence used to tease and bully a boy at his school. Lawrence and his friends picked on him just because he was different from them. He was short and his skin was a different colour from theirs. They used to taunt him all the time, calling him nasty names. Lawrence and his group could not pronounce the boy's name properly so they just called him Paki, even though his family did not come from Pakistan.

▲ Lawrence found it easy to become part of a group of bullies. His gang liked to pick on people for fun.

Some days, Lawrence thought he might leave the boy alone, but his friends would start teasing the boy and Lawrence soon joined in. The boy used to look miserable most of the time and once they found him crying in the toilets. Lawrence and his friends found this really funny and teased him

22

even more. They were really horrible to him, and they got away with it because the teachers did not notice anything. They would take his lunch money off him and rip up his books in the school corridors. The boy was very quiet and just put up with it.

One day, Lawrence's English teacher said that she wanted to read out an essay written by one of the pupils. It was the story of a boy who was bullied by a gang in his school. It explained his feelings of unhappiness. It also described how he was punished at home by his parents for having torn his books and his clothes, even though it had been the gang's fault. The boy wrote about how he felt when he woke up each morning and realized that he would have to go to school again. His essay made Lawrence realize what effects bullying could have on someone. He had never thought of it from the boy's side before.

◀ Lawrence, along with the gang, made life miserable for the boy at breaktimes. They did not think about how afraid and unhappy he felt until they heard his story.

Lawrence thought about the boy a lot after the essay and felt horrible for what he had done to him. His friends felt the same way. To them it had been fun to tease the boy. They had all felt powerful and strong because he was so much smaller than them, but now they knew how he felt. Lawrence felt very ashamed. The boy had not even named any of them in his essay, and for that Lawrence was grateful. They all decided to stop picking on him.

▶ The teacher made it clear that she was angry and disappointed with the bullies in the boy's essay. Lawrence felt very guilty and ashamed.

Lawrence and his friends realized that it must have taken guts to write that essay about his feelings. The teacher thought that the boy's writing was brilliant and he got a really good mark for it.

Bullies are often fearful, jealous, cruel, angry and unhappy people. If you are a bully, you

◀ If you are a bully, try to understand why you want to be aggressive to others. It is much better to be friendly and happy with other children, as they will be friendly and cheerful back.

need to take a good look at yourself and ask: 'Why am I doing this? Why do I want to make this other person feel so bad? Is doing that going to make me feel good? What can I do to make me feel better about myself? Why can't I just be peaceful and leave people alone? I would like people to like me for myself, not because they are terrified of me.'

Once you have learned to stop making someone's life miserable, you should try to say sorry to them and try to replace anything you have stolen or broken. You should stop and think about the reason for your anger instead of just bullying someone. If you can begin to understand the cause of your anger, you can do something about it. Look at other children having fun and being friends together without the need to bully.

Julie's story

Julie was ten years old when she started to get bullied. There were two girls who ganged up on her at school and made her life a misery. Julie has no idea why, as she had done nothing to them.

They used to take her jacket from the cloakroom and hide it somewhere. Then they jumbled up her books. They even used to hit Julie on the head with a ruler when the teacher had her back

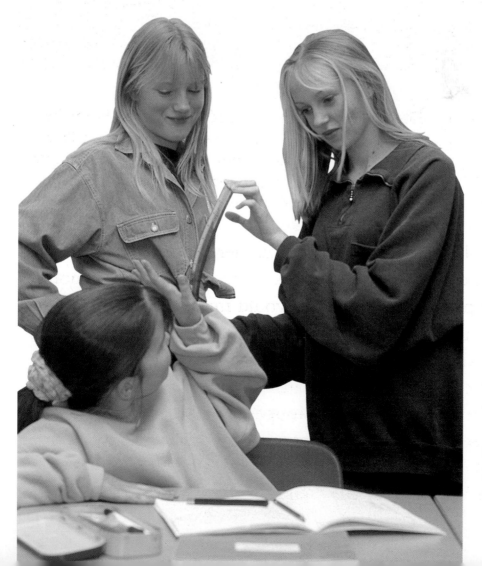

◀ Julie was bullied by two girls at her school for no reason that she knew. They would take her things, muddle up her books and even hit her on the head with a ruler.

turned to the class. If Julie had to get up during class, one of them would put her foot out to trip her up. They used to laugh at Julie and point at her on the way to and from school. It was dreadful. Julie felt especially bad when this caused people around her to look at her and wonder what was so odd about her.

Nothing they did seemed really bad but they made Julie feel awful. She told her mum about it and her mum spoke to the class teacher. Julie told her mum to tell

▲ Julie was often followed home by the two bullies who made her life a misery. They stopped when Julie told her mum about what a bad time she was having at school.

the teacher not to talk to the two girls about it because she thought it would make them worse. Julie does not know exactly what happened, and she never found out. But all the horrible things stopped as soon as her mum had been to the school. Nothing more happened and the two girls never said anything more to her.

Asking for help

If you are being bullied, tell your parents or an adult you trust. If you feel that you cannot talk to anyone, call one of the helpline numbers on page 31. Talk with them about what is best to do. You can talk to your class teacher or head teacher about it, or someone can talk to one of them for you.

Do not be afraid of sneaking, telling tales or 'grassing' on your bully. Your teachers and parents know that this may cause more trouble for you. They will not want you to be hurt any more, so they won't say or do anything to the bully if you do not want them to.

You will feel stronger and better about yourself as soon as you have told someone. Keeping the problem to yourself is the worst thing you can do.

◀ The first step towards looking after yourself is having the courage to tell someone that you are being bullied. If no one knows, no one can help you. Once you have some support, your life will quickly get better.

◀ Telling one of your parents that you are being bullied is the best way to start getting help. After that, it will be easier to talk to your class teacher. She will know how best to help you.

If you agree that your teacher should speak to the bully, he or she should be able to stop it happening again and make sure that you are safe. The bully's parents will be told and they will try to make the bully understand that his or her behaviour cannot be allowed. They may even try to take back your possessions or money from the bully. The bully may be punished at school, and certainly he or she will be watched very closely to make sure that it does not happen again.

Remember, if you allow your teacher to speak to the bully or bullies, the bullying will stop and your life will be better. If you do nothing, the bullying may get worse. Also, if you do and say nothing, the bully will have scored another victory over you. He or she will escape without punishment.

> **If you are being bullied:**
> **Do not put up with it.**
> **Tell someone.**
> **Ask that person to promise to tell you what they plan to do.**

Glossary

Aggression An attack without reason or cause.

Ashamed To feel bad about something you may have done or said.

Asthma A disorder in which the sufferer finds it difficult to breathe, and wheezes and feels a tightness in the chest.

Defend To avoid attack.

Depression A state in which you feel sad, lonely, anxious and believe that life is hardly worth living.

Eczema A skin disease in which the skin is red and raised with little bumps, and feels itchy and uncomfortable. The skin may flake off in places.

Insecure Always worried about danger or loss, and feeling unsafe, uncertain and nervous.

Jealousy A condition in which you fear, often for no reason, that something or someone is about to be taken away from you.

Physical Concerned with the body rather than the mind.

Possessions The things that belong to you, for example books, clothes and toys.

Psychiatrist A qualified medical doctor who tries to understand people's feelings so that he or she can help them to feel better.

Psychological When something affects how you feel and think.

Revenge To hurt or injure someone in return for something that they may have done or said to you.

Rumour A vague story that may or may not be true, which is told to a few people .

Self-confidence Feeling safe and strong enough to make and carry out your own decisions.

Taunt To make cruel or hurtful comments, to call names.

Tease To irritate, joke or to say nasty things.

Victim A person who is treated badly.

Further information

Books to read

Dealing with Bullying by John Coleman and Yvette Solomon, (Wayland, 1994)

Don't Pick on Me, How to Handle Bullying by Rosemary Stones,
  (Piccadilly Press, 1993)

The Bullying Problem: How to Deal with Difficult Children by Alan Train,
  (Souvenir Press, 1995)

Why Me? by Mary Morris and Sally MacLeod, (ChildLine, London, 1996)

What Do You Know about Bullying by Pete Sanders,
  (Gloucester Press, London 1993)

What's Happening? Bullying by Karen Bryant-Mole, (Wayland, 1994)

Booklets and leaflets

Anti Bullying Campaign (ABC), *Fact Sheets & Fact Pack*,(see useful addresses)

J. Balding, D. Regis, A. Wise, D. Bish and J. Muirden, *Bully Off*, (Schools Health Education Unit, University of Exeter, 1996)

Childline and Kidscape: various leaflets (see useful addresses)

Useful addresses

Anti Bullying Campaign (ABC), 10 Borough High Street, London SE1 9QQ
Tel: 0171 378 1446

ChildLine, Royal Mail Building, Studd Street, London N1 0QW
Tel: 0171 239 1000   0800 1111 (Free helpline)

Health Education Authority, Hamilton House, Mabledon Place,
London WC1H 9TX   Tel: 0171 383 3833

Kidscape, 152 Buckingham Palace Road, London SW1W 9TR
Tel: 0171 730 3300

National Society for the Prevention of Cruelty to Children (NSPCC)
42 Curtain Road, London EC2A 3NH
Tel: 0171 825 2500   0800 800 500 (Free helpline)

Young Minds Trust, 102/108 Clerkenwell Road, London EC1M 5SA
Tel: 0171 336 8445   0345 626376 (helpline)

Index